NO EASY WAY IN

OUT
OUT
WAY
WAY
EASY
EASY
ON
ON

ANDREW TARLOW

photographs **JULIA GILLARD**

recipes **CAROLINE FIDANZA**

art direction **BECKY JOHNSON**

Thank You   Thank You   Thank You

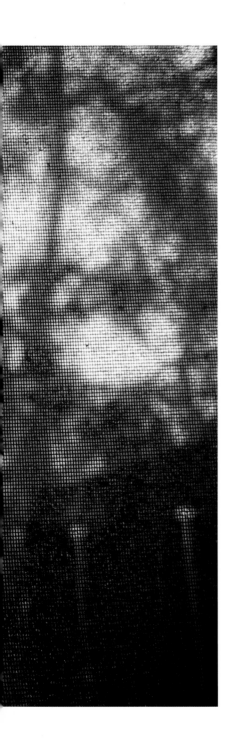

Thank You A.D. for
setting this book
in motion and
always being a ~~sound~~
source of inspiration.

Thank you Kate.
Since I got the
keys you have
propped me up
and inspired this
whole story.

Thank you Caroline
and Mark. I wouldn't
be here with out you.

Thank you Julia
for capturing the
light and the life.

Thank you Becky
for being the
majic eye.

Thanks to everyone
who works, worked,
eats, ate, drinks, drank
or showed up here at
this corner. You have
all made my dreams
come true.

A.T.

All photographs taken by Julia Gillard,
with the exception of the 3 vintage photos,
between 2010—2023 on the corner of
Broadway and Berry.

TEN SPEED PRESS

California | New York

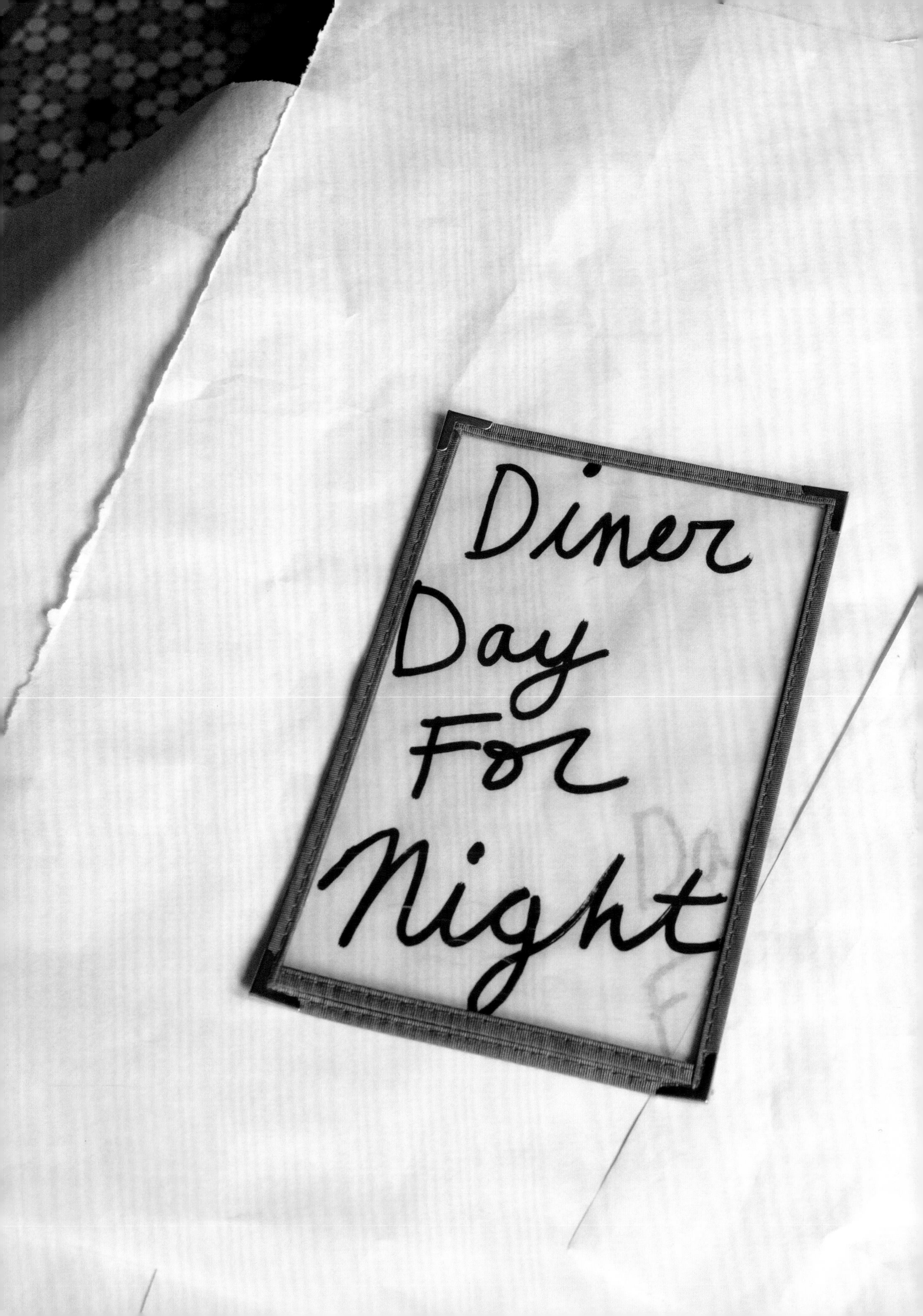
Diner
Day
For
Night

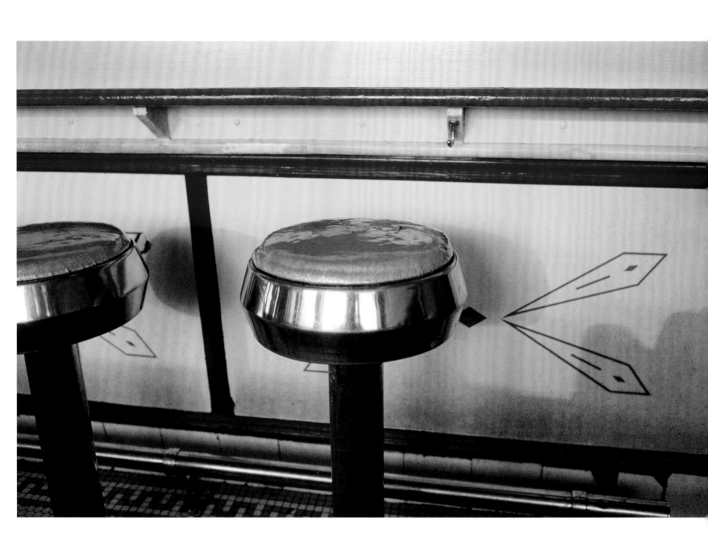

NYE
1998 into 1999

CAROLINE FIDANZA

Where did they all come from? My sister was in town, she came for the opening. I didn't think or know to invite anyone else. Randomly, a friend of hers visiting from SF found his way there too in spite of a vague invite and direction from Jackie . . . it's under the Williamsburg Bridge . . .

In 1998/1999 you didn't just take the L train over and walk south. For those of us who only took the train to Bedford, no one knew to ride the JMZ. And the G, I remember someone telling me they taught themselves how to tap dance waiting for it. A cab? They don't go over the bridge unless you close the door and hold in the destination until the car starts moving. You need to know to tell them to take the first exit and go all the way around in a U-turn down Broadway.

So, if you wanted to find Diner, you had to be prepared to find it. It required an old-fashioned sense of direction-based navigational skill and a stroke of good fortune. Also, dress warm, because there will be a lot of walking. Unless you live in the Gretsch Building, there's no way to get back from where you came at 3am that doesn't involve some time on foot and more likely, you're probably walking the whole way home. And it was always so cold on NYE.

In addition to Jackie and her friend Charles, there were about one thousand people. Without exaggeration three hundred. How did they know? I barely knew and I worked there. How many girlfriends did Mark Firth have? The place was stuffed with people.

Anything I remember about the rest of the night after we opened the bar is based on a photo I have of me and Jackie. We are both happy, clearly drunk, in the crowd with flutes of champagne. If I didn't have that photo I would only remember the cassoulet and the fact that the upstairs neighbor brought a cake, which I was annoyed by because I had already made a fantastic cake, chocolate soaked with rum, so I shoved his in the kitchen. Later, after everyone left, we ate it.

I first met AT in the summer of 1998. He interviewed me in his unairconditioned loft on a 98 degree August day in a part of Williamsburg I was always told to stay away from—which was basically anything south of Metropolitan Avenue. He served me a cup of hot tea, sat me on a stool in the middle of his huge and empty living room, and talked about his idea of opening a restaurant up the street which would serve eggs all day, while I sat there soaked. I remember the specific shirt and pants I was wearing and knew that I wasn't making much of an impression. I heard back from him a few months later when he still hadn't found anyone more suitable than me to consider for the job. This time he had Mark Firth with him. It was fall and it was a much friendlier meeting. I had been to France over the summer and saw all of the food that I had studied in cookbooks, in real life, before me. I was excited to make rillettes and rillons, braised lamb, butter lettuces with goat cheese, every kind of pork dish with mustard and cornichons. Mark immediately jumped in and started to rattle off all of the things he would love to serve in the restaurant. We still opened with a griddled ham and cheese and an egg sandwich on the menu but this was not where we were headed.

On NYE 1998 into 1999, I still didn't really know Andrew and Mark or any of their friends. I was there, but more as an observer than a participant. It was the first night of the job that would define the rest of my life, but it was other people's party. I had spent a little time helping get the restaurant opened. I painted the walk-in floor with Kate and went to restaurant supply with Andrew but with the gas off and the restaurant incomplete until we were ready to go, there wasn't that much I could do to prepare. I hadn't made any food until the cassoulet, which I assembled and heated at the loft reassured that maybe these guys weren't so bad after my introduction to South African Mark, who was so delighted by the preparations that had entered his home, providing his uniquely poetic narrative of every sensory experience bubbling under his nose and giving me the confidence that I was making the right decision to carry that pot up the block and into the future.

It was a week between the cassoulet and getting the gas turned on. The opening kitchen crew was me, Kate Huling, and Amanda Cole, Ken Reynold's girlfriend who helped with the construction in exchange for a job. Both Kate and Amanda were naturals in the kitchen. Amanda was opinionated and confident and it was she who figured out how to make a burger (I had never actually made one before). Kate was as happy to be in the kitchen as she was to be on the floor, doing whatever needed to be done to help. She made the chocolate Nemesis every day and was quite skilled at making big salads dressed with plenty of vinaigrette.

Andrew and Mark continued with their repairs and tweaks to the space by day and at night went home, showered, and returned decked out in suits and slicked-back hair. I was amused and a little baffled by their choice to overdress the part but realized after the fact that this was a very smart move, providing a clubby air that was not quite exclusive but made you feel like you were somewhere, not just another Williamsburg cafe with mismatched tables and chairs. It declared them your hosts, you were in their place, and they were going to show you a good time.

Having opened on NYE means that every anniversary is the biggest night of the year. It's a double celebration of and in a place that was already living every day pretty well to the max. It also became sort of a neighborhood anniversary. A central point in the story of many. It was epic and it still holds the power to be that place twenty-five years later.

It would be impossible to speak to all of the people who have passed through this restaurant. I'd love to try to make a list, but I could never remember everyone, and I'd hate to forget anyone. But what is true for most of them is that they each brought something with them that led us, one by one, onward. This space holds their stories in its story. It's impossible to speak about Diner without speaking of the past. It bridges us to another time in another city but also inspires us to keep recreating this space with these people and to keep moving forward.

BROOKLYN:
MY PART IN ITS DOWNFALL

MARK FIRTH

Diner wasn't the first diner we looked at once Andrew and I had decided to open our own restaurant. We were working at Odeon and Balthazar respectively and lived in a six-thousand-square-foot loft at 35 Broadway, rented from Isaac, an Israeli taxi medallion owner and car mechanic who owned half the neighborhood. He was a cross between Al Pacino and Robert De Niro but with dirty fingernails. The loft was basically a catalyst for everything that happened and everyone we met before we opened the restaurant. We rented it out for movies, music videos, and fashion shoots and threw parties with abandon. The space was perfect, with a pool table, axe throwing range, and enough room for roller blading and ping pong. The police would show up and the whole party would hide in the back studio until they left. We found Ken Reynolds sleeping on one of the many couches that we had in various areas around the loft (who knows how long he had been there), but he had an Irish glint in his eye and a can-do attitude that made us fast friends.

We had our eyes on a gleaming stainless-steel behemoth of a diner on Wythe Avenue across the street from Slicks motorcycle shop. The seventy-five-ish-year-old owner showed us he could still "hang with the kids" by dropping down and banging out twenty-five push-ups before he had Andrew sit on his back and do a few more. However, it turned out the money offered by the next prospective renters was worth more than our CrossFit games bonding. Disappointed, we turned to the more modest yellow faux-bricked facade of 85 Broadway. It had been sitting quiet for at least three or four years.

We set up a meeting with the son of the building's owner, Ray Jr. His father Ray Sr. ran it as a diner in the '70s and was infamous for his Colt 45 and large frame wedged behind the granite topped counter. Ray Jr. opened the battered old steel door and crept in slowly, as if he didn't want to disturb the ghosts of a thousand mice. "Did you hear that?" he said as he whipped out a snub-nosed revolver and spun into the room. All we could see were Formica tables and a Coke machine that was now an SRO for cockroaches. Despite the layers of grease and dirt, we were smitten. We convinced Isaac to buy the building, give us a lease, and set about renovating the place. The first thing we did was take down the old siding behind the bar, discovering rows of original subway tile that we put aside for later. We then screwed up a piece of Sheetrock and scrawled "Build it and they will come." And then, as two bartenders who could barely swing a hammer, we were stuck. Fortunately, our new friend Ken Reynolds—who's first words when he saw our handy work were, "Well, that is not going to fly"—took the Sheetrock down.

After that we were on a roll, Ken in charge, hiring our roommates, ex-girlfriends, neighbors, and welders to help tile, paint, and clean while we each held down three jobs. I risked deportation to hang drapes in Vancouver so we could afford an ice machine. We begged, borrowed, and not quite stole from our friends and family, and after six months we were almost there.

All we needed was a chef. We struck gold with Caroline—when she showed up with one eyebrow raised to help finish the kitchen and get us ready to open, I could tell that she was thinking, *What the hell have I agreed to?* But she pushed us from day one, to buy better ingredients, to find more sustainable meat sources, and to make friends with the farmers—and soon they were delivering to us after the farmers' markets.

The first meal she ever cooked for us was opening night down the street at our loft. It was a cassoulet with a watercress salad that we ferried up to the restaurant in large pots. We invited all the people who had helped us to dinner and then everyone we knew (or had met the night before) for the party. We spent New Year's Eve running around, last-minute fixing, painting, stocking the bar, and filling bins with ice, wine, and beer (we didn't have a fridge). We all took turns to shower and get dressed up for the party. I found myself alone at the first booth, and I had a silent cry. I had left home when I was eighteen and had been unrooted for years, but finally this felt like home and my new family.

There was no Yelp or Instagram back then, so Diner spread through word of mouth. There was no one to listen to you yell into the void of the internet because we forgot your order, or the seats were cramped, or we refused to turn down the music on Tuesday nights. If you liked it, you came back, and a lot of people came back. We under-promised and over-delivered; the exterior was plain and dimly lit; people often paused outside, unsure, almost daring themselves to step inside. Once they did, they were met with a wall of loud music, even louder people, and food that was simple and delicious. I wouldn't change a thing.

GOOD
MORNING
MOON

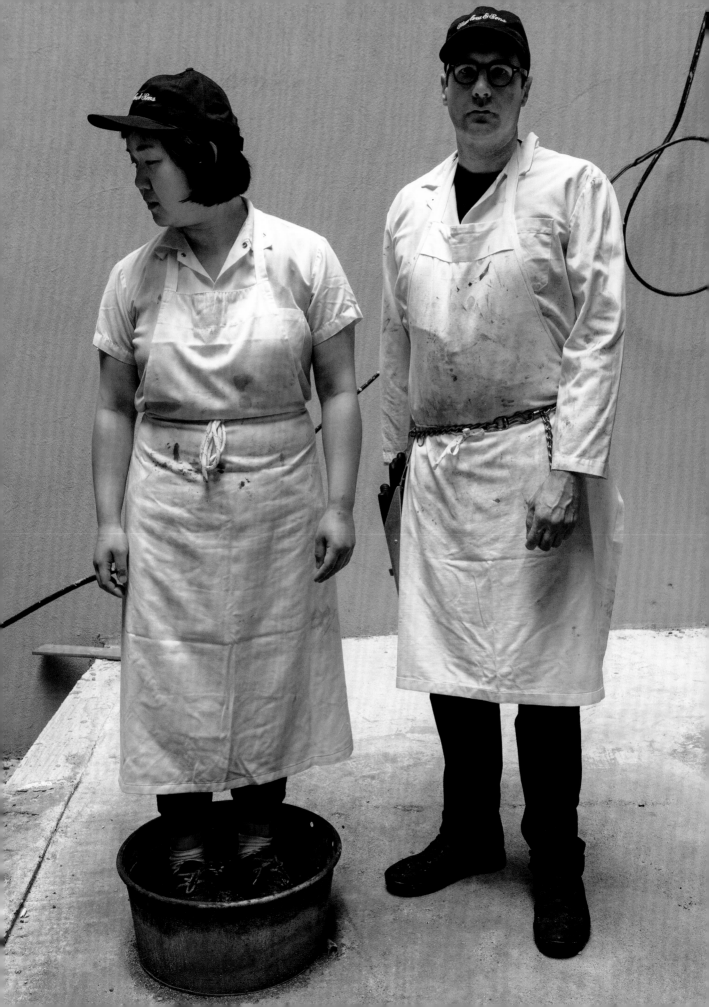

MIDDAY
MADE OF
MANY
MOMENTS

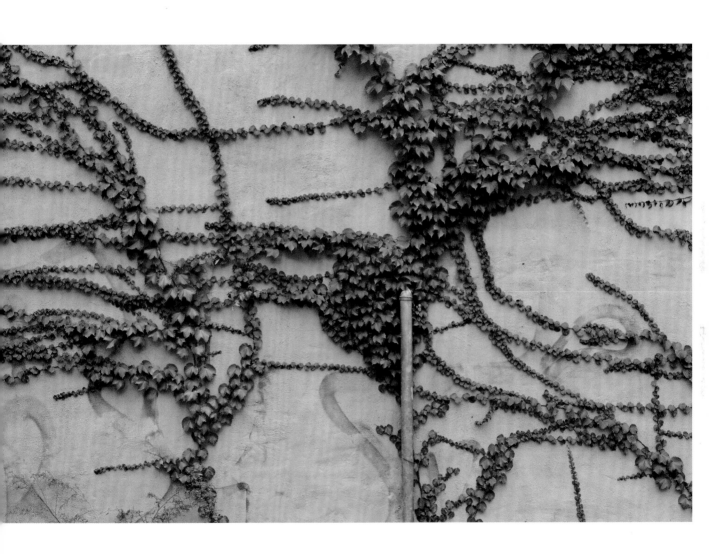

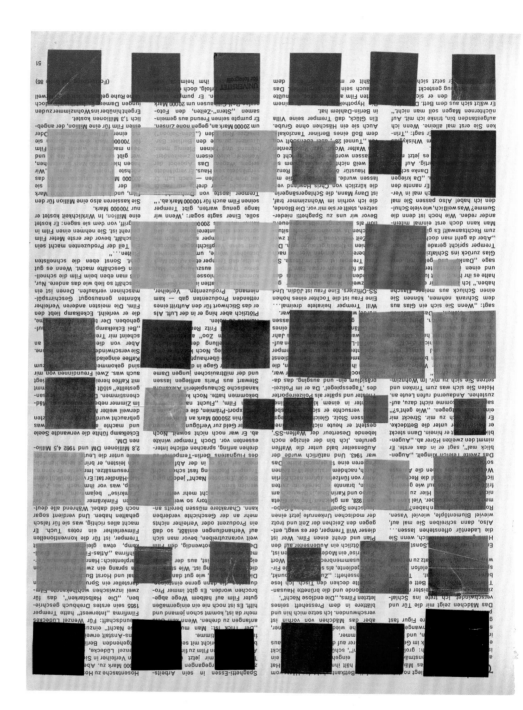

EVENING IN A ROOM WAITING FOR PEOPLE

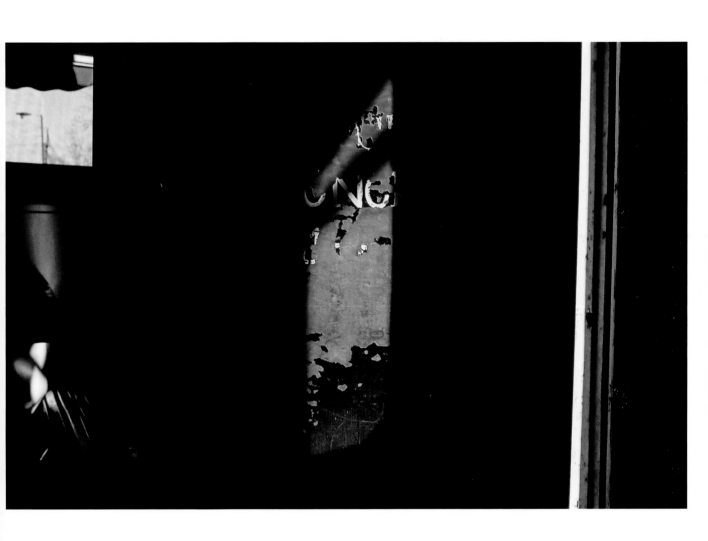

THE MIDDLE OF THE NIGHT HAS YOU IN IT

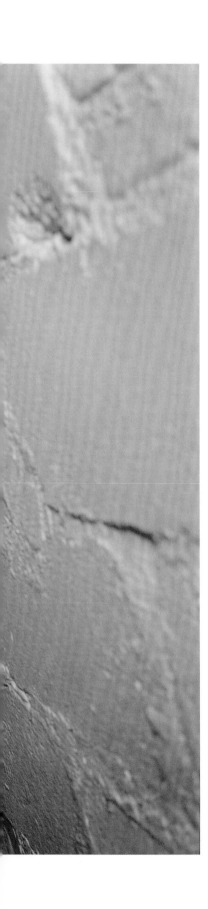

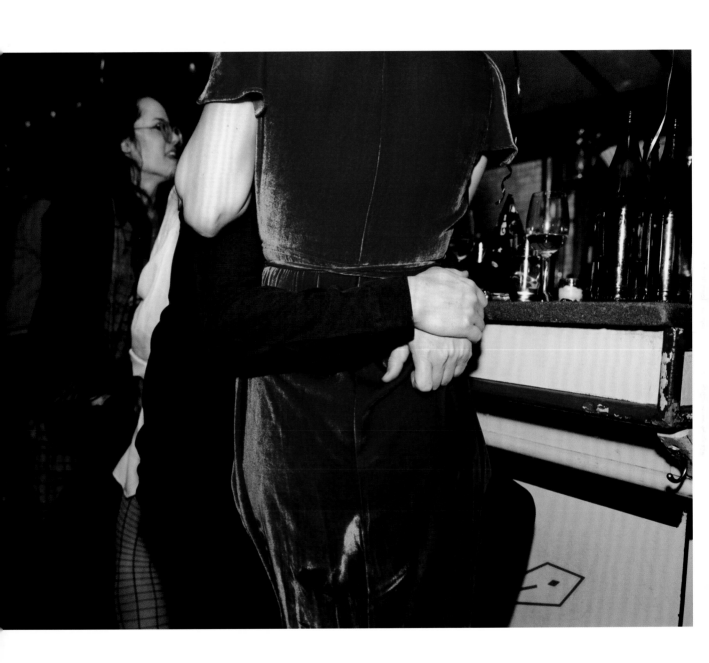

134

FOUR MENUS FOR FOUR TIMES OF THE YEAR

Many of these recipes were culled from diner journals or offered from chefs past and present. Thank you to all of you for your contributions to the pages here and for the inspired work over these many years.

—CF

TOAST
SPRING GREENS
PANZANELLA
ASPARAGUS
ARTICHOKES

BRAISED BEEF
SKATE
RiSOTTO
LAMB LEG STEAK
BRICK CHICKEN

CHERRY CLAFoUTIS
BASQUE CHEESECAKE

TOAST, hard-boiled egg, and ramp salsa verde

SERVES 4

4 eggs

1 bunch ramps, bulbs and greens separated

Extra-virgin olive oil

1 tablespoon capers in brine, chopped

2 to 3 tarragon sprigs, chopped

1 chile de árbol, crushed

1 lemon, zested and juiced

Sea salt

1 loaf sourdough or other excellent bread

8 ounces labne or crème fraîche, for serving

Prepare an ice bath. Boil the eggs in salted water for 7 minutes. Plunge the eggs into the ice bath and peel immediately. Hold at room temperature.

To make the salsa verde, slice the ramp bulbs and sauté in olive oil quickly just to soften. Remove the pan from the heat and toss in the ramp greens. Mix in the capers, tarragon, chile, and lemon zest. Season with salt, olive oil, and lemon juice. You want this mixture to be fairly oily, not dry at all.

Slice the bread into as many toasts as you want to eat. Heat a pan with a generous amount of olive oil and toast the bread in the pan until golden on both sides. Spread labne or crème fraîche onto the bread. Either chop and mix the eggs into the ramps (easier to eat) or place the ramp mixture on top of the labne and then finish it with halved or quartered eggs on top.

SPRING GREENS, soft herbs, and goat cheese

SERVES 2 TO 4 DEPENDING ON HOW MUCH SALAD YOU EAT

1 large head butter lettuce
or 2 heads Little Gem lettuce

1 teaspoon Dijon mustard

2 tablespoons white wine vinegar

4 tablespoons extra-virgin
olive oil

Sea salt

1 small bunch chives, finely sliced

12 mint leaves, picked

4 tarragon sprigs, picked

12 basil leaves

12 parsley leaves

1 bunch breakfast radishes,
left whole or sliced as you like

4 ounces fresh chèvre cheese

I like to keep the leaves whole for this; the lettuces can be used as a cup to hold the other ingredients.

Make a quick vinaigrette by dissolving the mustard into the vinegar and adding the olive oil and a pinch of salt. Stir the vinaigrette around before tossing it with the lettuce. Sprinkle the herbs and radishes on top of the greens and crumble the goat cheese all about the plated salad.

PANZANELLA, green garlic, arugula, and prosciutto

SERVES 4

MUSTARD VINAIGRETTE

1 teaspoon Dijon mustard

1 teaspoon whole-grain mustard

¼ cup champagne vinegar or white wine vinegar

½ cup extra-virgin olive oil

Kosher salt

SALAD

1 loaf good-quality bread

Extra-virgin olive oil

Sea salt

2 medium leeks (spring leeks are skinny, if you have those, use 4), thinly sliced from white to green until the greens feel tough

2 green garlic bulbs, thinly sliced

4 scallions, white and green parts, thinly sliced

1 bunch arugula, washed and spun

4 to 8 slices prosciutto or other delicious ham

Make the mustard vinaigrette by combining the Dijon mustard, whole-grain mustard, vinegar, olive oil, and salt. Set aside.

Cut the crust off the bread and tear the center of the bread into 1-inch pieces. Heat a large sauté pan and add a generous amount of olive oil. When the oil is warm, add the bread and season it with salt. Toss and toast the bread until it is golden brown but still chewy in the middle. Ideally, do this right before you are going to eat it, so the bread stays in its perfect state and doesn't get dry. Transfer the bread to a bowl.

In the same pan, lightly sauté the leeks and garlic until just soft. Transfer the leeks and garlic to the bowl with the bread and add the scallions and arugula. Toss everything with the vinaigrette and serve on top of sliced prosciutto or ham.

ASPARAGUS, tahini sauce, and wilted frilly mustard greens

SERVES 2 TO 4

1 bunch asparagus, tough ends removed

Kosher salt

½ cup high-quality tahini, such as Soom

1 to 2 lemons

1 bunch mixed medium-sized frilly spring mustard greens

Extra-virgin olive oil

Place the asparagus in a pan over high heat and cover two-thirds of the way with water. Sprinkle salt over the asparagus. When the water comes to a boil, cook for 3 minutes. Lift the asparagus out of the pan and drain.

Mix tahini in a bowl with a pinch of salt and the juice of half a lemon. Add water a couple of tablespoons at a time and thin the tahini to a hummus-like consistency. At first, the tahini will seize up, but as you add more water it will thin out and get creamy.

Spread the tahini sauce on the bottom of a serving plate. Place the asparagus on top of the sauce. Set aside.

In a bowl, dress the mustard greens well with salt, lemon juice, and olive oil. You can be aggressive dressing and mixing the greens, you want them to wilt a bit. Place the greens on top of the asparagus.

BRAISED ARTICHOKES, Sean's

SERVES 4

1 lemon

4 large artichokes

¼ cup extra-virgin olive oil

8 garlic cloves, thinly sliced

1 large onion, thinly sliced

1 large carrot, thinly sliced

Kosher salt

1 cup white wine

1 cup chicken stock

8 thyme sprigs

Large pinch saffron

Aioli or Dijonnaise (1 tablespoon Dijon mustard to 2 tablespoons mayonnaise), for serving

Put a quart of cold water into a bowl and squeeze the lemon into it. Peel and discard the tough outer leaves from the artichokes until you reach the yellow interior leaves. Lay the artichoke on a cutting board and cut off the green top half inch of leaves. Cut the artichoke in half lengthwise and remove the choke. Submerge the artichokes in the lemon water until ready to cook.

Preheat the oven to 350°F. Place the artichokes in a roasting pan with the interiors facing up. In a pan over medium heat, warm the olive oil, sizzle the garlic, then add the onion and carrot. Season well with salt and toss everything to combine. Add the wine and stock to the carrot and onion. Bring to a boil and pour the liquid with the carrots and onions over the artichokes.

Nestle in the thyme and cover the pan with foil. Bake for approximately 45 minutes, until the artichokes are knife tender.

Remove the pan from the oven and add the saffron to steep in the liquid as the artichokes cool.

Serve warm or chilled, with aioli or Dijonnaise.

BRAISED BEEF, roasted turnips, boiled potatoes, and mustard vinaigrette

SERVES 2

2 (2-inch-thick) crosscut beef shanks

Kosher salt

Pepper

Extra-virgin olive oil

8 small to medium new potatoes

1 bunch Hakurei turnips with nice tops, cut in half lengthwise

Mustard Vinaigrette (page 147)

Season the beef shanks well with salt and pepper. In a heavy pot over medium heat, warm 3 tablespoons of olive oil and brown the shanks on both sides. Once brown, pour off the oil from the shanks and add cold water to cover the shanks two-thirds of the way. Cover the pot, lower the heat to bring the water just to a simmer, and cook for 2 to 3 hours, adding water as necessary, until the shanks are tender.

Remove the pot from the heat. Let the shanks cool in their liquid. Once cool, pull the shank meat into spoon-sized pieces and reheat them in the broth they simmered in.

In a medium pot, boil the potatoes in salted water until tender. When cool enough to handle, peel the potatoes.

In a large cast-iron skillet over medium-low heat, warm about 4 tablespoons of olive oil and place the turnips cut side down evenly around the perimeter of the pan. Leave the greens outside of the pan. Cook the turnips until golden and tender. Once the turnips are cooked through, fold in the greens to just wilt.

Arrange the turnips, potatoes, and shank meat in a shallow bowl. Drizzle the mustard vinaigrette over the potatoes and turnips. Pour in some beef broth to fill the base of the bowl.

SKATE, skordalia, bronze fennel, and herb salad

SERVES 2

SKORDALIA

1 pound Yukon Gold potatoes

5 garlic cloves, pounded with sea salt in a mortar and pestle

¼ cup extra-virgin olive oil

¼ cup lemon juice

Kosher salt

HERB SALAD

½ cup loose-picked bronze fennel

½ cup loose-picked Italian flat-leaf parsley

½ cup loose-picked mint

1 small bunch chives, cut into 1-inch batons

4 scallions, thinly sliced

Sea salt

1 tablespoon lemon juice

3 tablespoons extra-virgin olive oil

1 (12-ounce) skate wing, bone-in, cut into 2 pieces

Kosher salt

Extra-virgin olive oil

1 tablespoon unsalted butter

To make the skordalia, boil the potatoes in a medium pot of well-salted water until tender. Drain the potatoes and cool them on a sheet tray. When they're cool enough to handle, peel the potatoes with a paring knife, and crumble them apart with your hands.

Place the garlic in the bowl of a food processor, and process to break the garlic down. Add the potatoes, and process. While the machine is running, add the olive oil in a steady stream followed by the lemon juice. Process until the potatoes are smooth, but don't overprocess them or they will become gummy. Season with salt and hold at room temperature.

Prepare a salad with the fennel, parsley, mint, chives, and scallions by tossing them with sea salt, lemon juice, and olive oil.

Season the skate well with kosher salt. Warm a heavy bottomed sauté pan with olive oil over medium-high heat. Place the skate in the oil and cook it until the skate browns. Flip the fish and brown on the other side. Depending on the thickness of your skate fillet, you will probably be able to cook it all the way on the stovetop, but if it's particularly large, you may need to put it in a hot oven at 425°F for a few minutes. Either way, once the skate is cooked, discard the oil you cooked the fish in and finish the skate by basting it in butter. Move the fillet to the middle of the pan, tilt the pan on the burner, add a tablespoon of butter to the bottom of the pan, and spoon the butter over the fish until the butter and fish turn a deep brown.

Place the skordalia on the plate and the skate on top of it. Spoon the browned butter over the fish and then the salad on top of the fish.

RISOTTO, leeks, peas, pea shoots, pecorino

SERVES 2 TO 4

¼ cup extra-virgin olive oil, plus more as needed

4 tablespoons unsalted butter

1 bunch leeks, white parts and tender green parts, diced

Kosher salt

1 cup arborio rice

2 cups white wine

2 quarts hot chicken or vegetable stock

2 cups shucked peas, blanched and shocked

4 ounces young Pecorino Toscano, half grated, half shaved

Bundle of pea shoots

¼ lemon

Warm the olive oil and butter in a wide pot over medium-high heat. Once the butter starts to sizzle, add the leeks. Season the leeks with salt and stir them around until they are well coated with oil and butter. Stir in the rice until it becomes sticky and toasty. Add the wine to the rice and lower the heat to medium, stirring the rice continuously until the wine starts to evaporate. As the wine evaporates, add the chicken stock, one ladle at a time, stirring frequently as the rice absorbs the liquid. Keep this going until all the chicken stock is used and the rice starts to release its starch and become creamy, about 25 minutes. Add the peas to warm them through then add the grated half of the pecorino, stirring so the cheese melts into the risotto. Taste the risotto for seasoning and add salt as needed.

Toss the pea shoots with a little olive oil and a squeeze of lemon. Serve the risotto with the shaved pecorino and pea shoots strewn about the top.

LAMB LEG STEAK, Swiss chard, and flageolet

SERVES 2

1 cup dried flageolet beans

Sea salt

Extra-virgin olive oil

Kosher salt

1 (1½-inch thick) crosscut lamb leg steak

1 bunch Swiss chard

1 tablespoon Dijon mustard

4 garlic cloves, thinly sliced

4 rosemary sprigs, picked

Soak the flageolet beans in water overnight. In a small pot, cook the beans in just enough water to cover them but not drown them, until tender. When cooked, season with sea salt and a round of extra-virgin olive oil. Let cool.

Season the lamb with kosher salt and cook on a hot grill until medium-rare or until a meat thermometer reads 125°F.

In a medium pan over medium-high heat, sauté the Swiss chard in olive oil until just wilted. Season the Swiss chard with kosher salt and stir in the Dijon mustard. Mix to dissolve the mustard. Remove the Swiss chard from the pan and set aside.

In the same pan, heat 3 tablespoons of olive oil and add the garlic. Cook the garlic until the slices are golden, then add the rosemary and cook for about a minute until it releases its aroma.

Spread the Swiss chard on a plate. With a slotted spoon, spoon the flageolet beans and some of the liquid onto the Swiss chard. Slice the lamb next to the beans and chard and spoon the garlic and rosemary mixture on top of the lamb.

BRICK CHICKEN,
spinach, and green garlic

SERVES 2

One half chicken

Kosher salt

¼ to ⅓ cup extra-virgin olive oil

Unsalted butter

1 bunch green garlic, thinly sliced

½ cup white wine

½ cup chicken stock

1 bunch large leafy spinach

½ lemon, juiced

A brick chicken is a boned-out, intact half chicken. If you are preparing the chicken yourself, start by cutting along the length of the breastbone. Then shift your knife horizontally to remove the meat from the bone as you move toward the side/back of the bird. Once you get to the point where the leg is in the way of your knife, cut the thigh from the bone where the hip socket lies (this whole thing is about staying along the bone). Pop out the hip socket and cut as far back as you can to maintain all the thigh. Continue slowly cutting the meat from the bone until you get all the way around to the back of the bird. Once the breast and leg are off the bone, cut the whole thing away from the carcass. Score the thigh bone with your knife and follow with the tip of your knife along and around that bone until you can cut it free from the thigh. Score the drumstick as well but leave the bone in. Remove the wing tip but leave the top of the wing.

Season the chicken well on both sides with salt. Heat a heavy-bottomed (ideally cast-iron) pan over high heat with enough oil to cover the bottom of the pan and place the chicken, skin side down, in the pan. Find something to weigh the chicken down with. This can be another pan that lies on top of the chicken with something heavy inside. Or you could use an actual brick as the recipe title suggests—just make sure to wrap it in aluminum foil first.

Turn the heat down to medium and let the chicken fry in the pan until the skin is very crispy and brown. You are essentially trying to cook the chicken most of the way on its skin side. Once nicely browned, flip the chicken and finish cooking on the flesh side. You can also put the chicken flesh-side down into a 400°F oven at this point for about 5 minutes. Make sure the chicken is cooked through (a meat thermometer will read 165°F) and that no blood is visible.

Remove the chicken from the pan and set aside. In the same pan over medium heat, add some butter and quickly cook the green garlic in the pan. Deglaze the pan with white wine and chicken stock.

Toss the spinach with a pinch of salt and the lemon juice and then place the spinach on a plate or platter. Pour the deglazed sauce with the green garlic over the spinach and eat alongside your brick chicken.

CHERRY CLAFOUTIS

SERVES 6

6 eggs

½ cup sugar

1 vanilla bean, scraped

1 cup milk

⅔ cup all-purpose flour

Pinch of salt

4 tablespoons unsalted butter, melted

1 pound sweet cherries, stemmed but not pitted

Powdered sugar, for serving

Preheat the oven to 400°F. Ideally, this clafoutis should be made in a cast-iron skillet, but if you don't have one, a round cake pan will do.

In a large mixing bowl, combine the eggs, sugar, and vanilla. Beat with an electric mixer until frothy. Slowly add in the milk, then gently mix in the flour, salt, and melted butter. Mix until the batter is fully incorporated.

Put the cherries on the bottom of the pan, pour the batter over the cherries, and bake until the clafoutis is golden brown and firm to the touch, about 30 minutes. Serve with powdered sugar.

BASQUE CHEESECAKE

SERVES 10 TO 12

4½ cups cream cheese, room temperature

1¾ cups sugar

2 cups heavy cream

3 tablespoons all-purpose flour

6 eggs

1 egg yolk

1 teaspoon vanilla extract

Zest of 1 orange

Preheat the oven to 450°F. Line a 9-inch springform pan with parchment paper.

Place the cream cheese and sugar in the bowl of an electric mixer and whip with the paddle attachment until light and fluffy.

In a separate bowl, whisk the heavy cream and flour together until completely blended. Add this to the cream cheese mixture and stir until there are no lumps, making sure not to overmix. Add the eggs and egg yolk in one at a time until well combined. Add the vanilla extract and orange zest. Stir to combine.

Pour the batter into the prepared pan and bake for 30 minutes, until black on top and ever so slightly jiggly in the middle. Remove the cake from the oven and cool in the pan for an hour before cooling it in the refrigerator uncovered for at least 4 hours.

We serve this cheesecake with rhubarb sauce, which is rhubarb cooked down in sugar. It would be great with any seasonal fruit but is truly not in need of any adornment—it's just so good as it is.

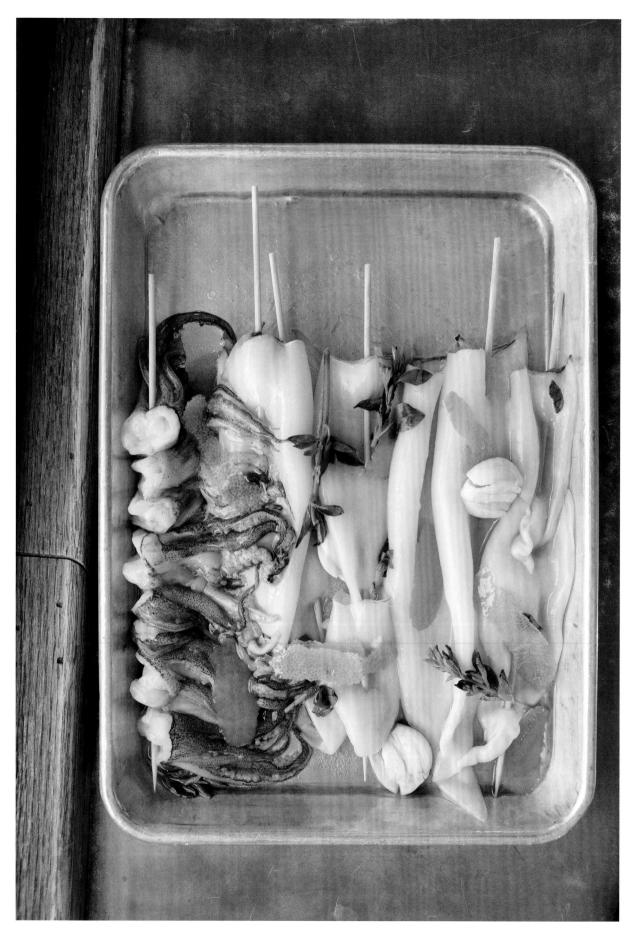

GREEN TOMATOES
TOAST
TOMATO ANCHOIADE
CLAMS
SQUID

WILD STRIPED BASS
BUTCHER'S STEAK
FLUKE
BLUEFISH
PORK SIRLOIN

PEACHES
OLIVE OIL CAKE

GREEN TOMATOES, mozzarella, basil, and green coriander

SERVES 2 TO 4

2 green unripe tomatoes

Sea salt

3 tablespoons extra-virgin olive oil, plus more to add to the coriander seeds

2 tablespoons white wine vinegar

1 tablespoon fresh coriander seed

12 basil leaves

½ pound fresh mozzarella or burrata, torn into chunks

Thinly slice the green tomatoes and sprinkle with sea salt until they start to soften. Once wilted, marinate the tomatoes in the olive oil and vinegar. Let sit for at least one hour.

Using a mortar and pestle, lightly pound the fresh coriander seeds to open them up. Add a little olive oil to the ground coriander seeds, mix well, and drizzle over the marinated green tomatoes. Arrange the tomatoes with basil and top with torn mozzarella.

173

TOAST
with soft cheese
and marinated peppers

MAKES 4 TOASTS

4 mixed sweet or slightly hot peppers such as bell, cubanelle, cornito rosso, Jimmy Nardello, pasilla, poblano, or paprika if you can find them

4 garlic cloves, sliced

2 tablespoons pine nuts

¼ cup golden raisins, soaked in white wine vinegar

1 tablespoon capers

Sea salt

4 slices sourdough bread

8 ounces soft cheese, such as labne, goat cheese, ricotta, or stracchino

Grill and blister the peppers over an open flame. Put them in a bowl and cover with plastic wrap. When they're cool enough to handle, peel the peppers and slice them into 1-inch thick strips. It's okay if a little skin sticks to the pepper, some can be hard to peel.

In a small pan over medium heat, sizzle the garlic until golden. Add the pine nuts and cook until toasty. Using a slotted spoon, lift the raisins out of the vinegar, add them along with the capers to the pan, and heat everything through.

Toss the peppers with the garlic, pine nut, raisin, and caper mixture. Season with salt. Toast the bread and spread a nice layer of cheese over it. Place a generous portion of peppers on top of the cheese and toast.

TOMATO ANCHOIADE
for everything

MAKES 1 QUART

2 large tomatoes

1 cup cherry tomatoes

6 to 8 anchovy fillets

1 garlic head, separated into cloves and peeled

1 bunch basil

Extra-virgin olive oil

Sea salt

Preheat the oven to 350°F.

Core the large tomatoes and cut into wedges or tear them apart if they are ripe enough. In a medium oven-safe pot, combine the cut tomatoes, cherry tomatoes, anchovy fillets, garlic cloves, and basil. Pour olive oil up to about an inch from the top of the tomatoes. Cover the pot with the lid or aluminum foil. Roast the tomatoes until the garlic is completely soft, about 45 minutes. Taste for seasoning and add sea salt as needed.

Once cooked, strain the mixture through a food mill to capture the tomato skins and basil stems. If you don't have a food mill, strain the tomato mixture through a colander or pulse it in a food processor.

Serve the anchoiade with anything and everything—bread, meats, cheese, vegetables, pasta, or any other grain. If you are eating this with bread, you can go heavier on the tomatoes. If you are using this as a sauce for grilled meat or vegetables, you can go heavier on the anchovies.

CLAMS,
roasted cherry tomatoes, rosemary, and smoked paprika

SERVES 2 TO 4

24 littleneck clams

1 cup cherry tomatoes

Extra-virgin olive oil

Sea salt

4 garlic cloves, sliced

4 rosemary sprigs

½ teaspoon smoked paprika

1 cup white wine or sherry

2 tablespoons unsalted butter

Clean the clams well by soaking them in water so that they purge their sand. If they release a lot of grit, rinse and repeat the process, changing the water until the clams seem clean. Once soaked, scrub each clam under running water and then rinse and purge again.

Meanwhile, place the cherry tomatoes on a sheet tray. Drizzle with a little olive oil and a sprinkle of salt. Place the tomatoes under the broiler until they start to char and wilt, about 5 minutes. Set aside.

Heat a large pan with 2 tablespoons of olive oil. Add the garlic and cook until golden. Add the rosemary and the smoked paprika, allowing them to bloom in the oil before adding the clams. Toss the clams around in the pan to coat with the oil and seasonings. Add the white wine. Cover the pan and cook until the clams open. Once the clams have popped (toss any clams that haven't opened), add the butter and toss in the charred cherry tomatoes. Serve hot.

GRILLED SQUID,
bread crumbs, and salmoriglio

SERVES 4

¼ cup bread crumbs, ideally homemade

1 pound fresh, preferably dirty (unwashed) squid

Extra-virgin olive oil

4 garlic cloves, smashed

4 oregano sprigs, picked

Peel of 1 lemon

Peel of 1 orange

SALMORIGLIO

3 to 4 garlic cloves, smashed

Sea salt

1 bunch oregano, picked

½ cup extra-virgin olive oil

Kosher salt

Lemon wedges, for serving

Make your own bread crumbs from good-quality bread by slicing and toasting the bread, then pulsing it into rough crumbs in a food processor.

Pull the heads from the squid bodies. Cut off and save the tentacles just above the eyes, making sure to remove the "beak" that sits in that pocket. Stick your finger into the body of the squid, cleaning out anything that's inside, and rinse both the squid bodies and tentacles well under cold running water. Drain and pat with paper towels.

Soak 12-inch wooden skewers in water so they don't splinter. Once soaked, skewer the squid, making sure to leave at least 3 to 4 inches of space at the bottom. Don't over-pack the skewer; you'll want the squid to get a good char on it. Marinate the squid in ¼ cup of olive oil, garlic, oregano, lemon peel, and orange peel for one hour.

Make the salmoriglio. Using a mortar and pestle, pound the garlic with a teaspoon of sea salt. Once combined, add the oregano a little at a time, pounding until you achieve a smooth and even consistency. (If you don't have a mortar and pestle, you could use a food processor or knife to finely chop the ingredients.) Transfer the garlic and oregano mixture to a small pot and cover with the olive oil. Cook on very low for about 10 minutes. Salmoriglio can be made a day ahead of time, stored in the fridge, and brought to room temperature when ready to use.

When you are ready to grill the squid, season it all over with kosher salt. Cook it on a hot grill until nicely charred and opaque. Squeeze lemon on the squid when it comes off the grill and sprinkle bread crumbs on top while it's still hot. Drizzle the salmoriglio over the squid and eat right away.

WILD STRIPED BASS, sweet corn succotash

SERVES 4

1 cup shelled cranberry, lima, or other fresh bean

Kosher salt

Extra-virgin olive oil

4 garlic cloves, sliced

2 tablespoons unsalted butter

2 ears sweet corn, kernels cut off the cob

1 cup cherry tomatoes

1 cup ¼-inch okra pieces

½ cup heavy cream

1 bunch scallions, white and green parts, thinly sliced

2 dozen basil leaves

1½ pounds fresh wild striped bass, cut into 6-ounce pieces

In a small pot, cook the shell beans at a simmer in enough water just to cover them for about 30 minutes, until tender. Season with salt and a round of olive oil. Hold the beans in their liquid. If they get cold, warm them through again.

To make the succotash, in a medium pan over medium heat, cook the garlic in 2 tablespoons of olive oil and the butter. Once the garlic starts to turn golden, add the corn and adjust the heat to high. Season the corn with salt. Cook until the corn is a little toasty. Add the cherry tomatoes until they burst and then add the okra and more salt, cooking until the okra just loses its rawness but isn't mushy. (All of this should cook fast and hot.) Once everything has been sautéed, add the shell beans and turn the heat to low. Pour in the cream just to warm it through and add the scallions. Give everything a stir, toss in the basil, and set aside until ready to serve with the fish.

Season the flesh side of the fish with kosher salt. In a medium pan over medium heat, warm ¼ cup of olive oil and place the fish in the pan skin side down. Push the fish fillets down with the back of a spatula to get the skin to brown evenly. Once the skin is brown, either flip the fish and finish cooking it in the pan or put the fish into a 400°F oven for 3 to 4 minutes.

Serve the fish on top of the sweet corn succotash.

GRILLED BUTCHER'S STEAK, Denis Spina's eggplant and ricotta salata

SERVES 2 TO 4

1 large eggplant

Kosher salt

¼ cup extra-virgin olive oil, plus more as needed

2 leeks, white and tender green parts, sliced lengthwise and into 4-inch pieces

3 garlic cloves, smashed into pieces

1 teaspoon Aleppo pepper

1 tablespoon salt-packed capers, soaked in water and then drained

1 tablespoon red wine vinegar

Squeeze of lemon

1 pound "butcher's" steak (we prefer a bistro steak but any other cut would work)

Black pepper

4 ounces ricotta salata

Cut the top off the eggplant and slice lengthwise into ½-inch cutlets. Lay the eggplant slices out on a plate, sprinkle with salt, and let sit for an hour so that the eggplant starts to release its water.

Preheat the oven to 350°F. Oil a baking sheet.

Pat the eggplant dry, and lay it out on the oiled baking sheet. Add the leeks and the garlic to the sheet pan with the eggplant. Drizzle everything with olive oil, season with salt, toss it around with your hands, and lay everything in a single layer to roast.

Bake the eggplant until it is brown and soft, about 30 minutes. Remove the eggplant from the oven and toss with Aleppo pepper, capers, red wine vinegar, and lemon juice.

To cook the steak, season the steak well with salt and pepper. Heat a cast-iron skillet until smoking hot. Add ¼ cup of olive oil, place the steak into the pan, and cook until it is caramelized on one side. Flip the steak and cook it on the other side until well caramelized, or until a meat thermometer reads 135°F. The timing of caramelization to doneness should match up nicely if your steak is thick enough. Let the steak rest well before slicing. Plate the sliced steak with the eggplant, and shave the ricotta salata over both when ready to serve.

FLUKE "MILANESE," melted zucchini, cherry tomatoes

SERVES 4

1 cup all-purpose flour

Kosher salt

3 eggs, whisked

2 cups panko or bread crumbs

4 (4- to 6-ounce) fluke fillets

½ cup extra-virgin olive oil

Lemon wedges, for serving

MELTED ZUCCHINI

3 tablespoons extra-virgin olive oil

6 garlic cloves, sliced

2 medium zucchini, sliced ¼-inch thick

Kosher salt

1 pound cherry tomatoes

1 cup basil leaves

Set up a dredging station. Fill three bowls, one with flour and a teaspoon salt, one with the whisked eggs, and one with the panko. Dredge each fillet of fluke in the flour, shaking off any excess, then in the egg, then in the panko.

In a pan over medium-high heat, warm ½ cup of olive oil. When the oil starts to smoke, carefully place the fluke fillets, two at a time, in the pan and cook until golden on both sides. Remove the fluke from the pan and place the fish on a wire rack or paper towel until all the fillets are cooked. Season with salt as the fish comes out of the pan.

To make the melted zucchini, in a wide pot or sauté pan over medium heat, warm 3 tablespoons of the olive oil. Add the garlic until it sizzles and turns golden. Add the zucchini and toss it in the pan with the olive oil and garlic, season with salt, and allow the zucchini to get some color. Add the cherry tomatoes and cover the pot. Lower the heat to medium-low and cook until the zucchini and tomatoes melt. Toss in the basil.

Plate the fish and serve with a squeeze of lemon and the melted zucchini. (This also makes a great fish sandwich.)

BLUEFISH, chopped summer salad, yogurt, and sumac sprinkle

SERVES 4

1½ pounds bluefish fillet

Kosher salt

Extra-virgin olive oil

SUMMER SALAD

1 large shallot, thinly sliced

3 tablespoons white wine vinegar

1 large tomato

1 cucumber (lemon, Japanese white [Itachi], or Indian would be best)

¼ cup sliced Pickled Peppers (page 202)

Sea salt

3 tablespoons extra-virgin olive oil

1 small bunch purslane or arugula

YOGURT

1 cup yogurt

2 tablespoons toasted sesame seeds

1 tablespoon sumac

1 tablespoon Aleppo pepper

Pinch sea salt

Preheat the oven to 375°F.

Season the flesh side of the bluefish with salt. Spread 2 tablespoons of olive oil in the center of a sheet tray and lay the bluefish, skin side down, directly on the olive oil in the tray. Drizzle more olive oil on top of the fish and bake until cooked through, 10 to 20 minutes depending on the thickness of the fish.

To make the summer salad, put the shallot slices in a bowl, and cover with the white wine vinegar to marinate while assembling the rest of the salad.

Slice the tomato into wedges and the cucumber into ½-inch rounds (if the cucumber is round, cut it into wedges). Toss the Pickled Peppers with the tomato and cucumber. Add the shallot and the vinegar to the salad. Add a couple of pinches of sea salt and the olive oil. Toss everything well and then top it off with the purslane.

To make the yogurt mix, first whisk the yogurt to smooth it out and remove any lumpiness. In a small bowl, mix together the sesame seeds, sumac, Aleppo pepper, and sea salt. Spread the yogurt on the side of a plate or bowl and generously sprinkle the seed-and-spice mix over the top. Serve the salad next to or on top of the yogurt mix, and serve with the cooked bluefish.

198

PORK SIRLOIN,
porchetta spice, broccolini, and pickled peppers

SERVES 2

PORCHETTA SPICE

1 teaspoon black peppercorn

1 teaspoon coriander seed

1 teaspoon fennel seed

1 whole chile de arbol

1 pound pork sirloin

Kosher salt

1 bunch broccolini

Zest and juice of half a lemon

1 garlic clove, grated

2 tablespoons extra-virgin olive oil

Pickled Peppers (recipe follows)

To make porchetta spice, using a mortar and pestle or spice grinder, grind the peppercorn, coriander seed, fennel seed, and chile de arbol.

Season the pork with salt and the porchetta spice. Grill it for 5 to 7 minutes per side, until it gets brown on both sides and reaches an internal temperature between 145°F and 150°F. The pork sirloin should cook through in the time it takes to cook it to a nice brown on both sides.

Bring a pot of salted water to a boil. Cook the broccolini for 3 minutes, lift it out of the water, and toss it in a bowl with lemon zest, lemon juice, garlic, and olive oil. If you prefer some char on the broccolini, forgo the boiling method and instead heat a pan with olive oil and sear it on high heat.

Slice the pork and plate it with the broccolini. Serve with sliced pickled peppers.

PICKLED PEPPERS

1 cup cider vinegar

½ cup sugar

¼ cup salt

1 quart ají dulce peppers or other small fruity sweet peppers, cut in half, stemmed, and seeded

In a pot over high heat, combine the vinegar, sugar, salt, and 1 cup water. Bring to a boil and cook until both the sugar and salt dissolve. In an airtight jar, pour the pickling mixture over the peppers. Let the peppers pickle at least overnight before using.

PEACHES,
crème fraîche, honey,
lavender shortbread sprinkle

SERVES 4

1 cup butter, softened

¾ cup sugar

1 egg yolk

1 teaspoon vanilla

2 cups all-purpose flour

½ teaspoon sea salt, pounded with a mortar and pestle

2 teaspoons fresh or dried lavender

4 ripe peaches

2 tablespoons honey

2 cups crème fraîche

To make the lavender shortbread, cream the butter and sugar in the bowl of an electric mixer. Add the egg yolk and vanilla and whisk until combined. Sift the flour, salt, and lavender into the mixture. Mix well until there are no lumps, and it forms a cohesive batter. Roll out the dough in a rectangular shape until it's ⅛-inch thick. Wrap and chill for an hour.

Preheat the oven to 350°F. Cut the dough into 2-inch squares and bake on a baking sheet for 10 minutes, until golden. When the shortbread is done, rest the pieces on a wire rack until cool enough to handle. Crumble the shortbread.

While the shortbread is baking, cut the peaches into wedges and toss them with honey. Let the peaches sit until they start to release a little of their juice, about half an hour.

Place the peaches in a bowl and spoon over a generous amount of crème fraîche. Sprinkle the lavender cookie crumbs on top of the bowl.

OLIVE OIL CAKE,
roasted apricots

SERVES 8 TO 10

1 cup extra-virgin olive oil,
plus more for the pan

1 cup cornmeal

1¾ cups almond flour

¾ teaspoon salt

2 teaspoons baking powder

1¼ cups sugar

5 eggs

Zest of 2 lemons

Zest of 1 orange

6 apricots, halved and pitted

4 tablespoons unsalted butter,
melted

2 tablespoons honey

Preheat the oven to 325°F. Oil a 9-inch round cake pan.

In a large bowl, whisk the cornmeal, almond flour, salt, and baking powder. In another large bowl, whisk the sugar, olive oil, eggs, lemon zest, and orange zest. Fold the dry ingredients into the wet ingredients and stir to incorporate. Pour the batter into the prepared cake pan, and bake for 35 minutes. Remove the cake from the oven, let cool slightly, and adjust the oven temperature to 375°F. Gently remove the cake from the pan when warm to the touch.

On a baking sheet, toss the apricots with the melted butter and honey and roast for 10 minutes, until they get a little brown and sticky.

Slice the cake and serve the apricots alongside it. Drizzle the apricots with their juice.

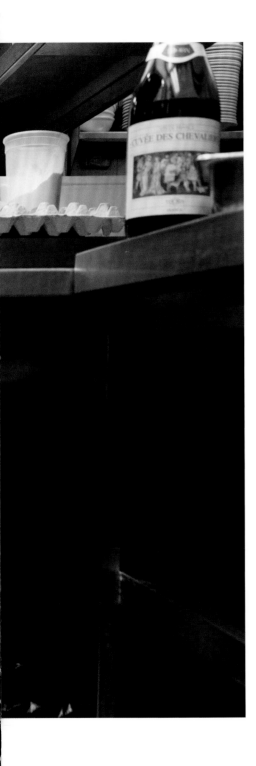

SARDINES ON TOAST
WHITE SALAD
PUMPKIN
TURNIPS + RADISHES
"MINESTRONE"

CHICKEN SCHNITZEL
POACHED CHICKEN
MEATBALLS
LAMB BELLY
PORK CHOP

GINGER CAKE
PLUMS

SARDINES ON TOAST,
aioli, celery, and radish

SERVES 4

8 fresh whole sardines

3 tablespoons extra-virgin olive oil, plus more for the pan

Sea salt

Lemon

SALAD

1 celery heart, tender ribs and leaves thinly sliced

4 French breakfast or red globe radishes (or whatever radish you prefer), julienned

½ small red onion or 3 scallions, sliced very thinly

3 tablespoons extra-virgin olive oil

½ lemon, juiced

Sea salt

AIOLI

1 egg yolk

1 garlic clove, minced or pounded in a mortar and pestle

2 teaspoons white wine vinegar

1 teaspoon kosher salt

1 cup olive pomace oil

Squeeze of lemon

Miche or sourdough bread, cut into four 4 by 1½-inch slices

Pinch Aleppo pepper

Prepare the sardines by running them under water to flake off the scales with the force of the tap. Once scaled, make an incision in the belly and run the fish under the tap. The water will loosen the guts and it should be easy to pull them out. Rinse well once removed. Lay the sardines on a cutting board and, using a small knife, cut the fillet off the bone. It's very easy to do this given that the fish is small and very soft. Sardine bones are edible so any pin bones are fine, but it's nice to try to get the long rib bones out.

Place the sardines skin side up on a baking tray. Drizzle them with olive oil and season them with salt. Put the tray of sardines under the broiler until the skin is golden and the fish opaque. Remove the sardines from the broiler and generously squeeze lemon over the sardines.

To make the salad, in a large bowl, mix the celery, radishes, and onion together. Dress with olive oil, lemon juice, and a pinch of sea salt.

To make the aioli, in the bowl of a food processor, place the egg yolk, garlic, vinegar, and salt. Pulse to combine. Slowly drizzle in the olive pomace oil. Thin with water as necessary. Season with a squeeze of lemon.

To prepare the toast, heat a cast-iron skillet with enough olive oil to evenly cover the bottom of the pan. Toast the bread in the pan until deeply golden and repeat on the other side.

Cover the toast with a generous layer of aioli. Place 2 to 3 sardine fillets on top of the aioli. Scoop a nice quantity of salad on top of the sardines and then sprinkle with Aleppo pepper.

WHITE SALAD,
cauliflower, fennel, cabbage, green olive, and salami

SERVES 4

1 bulb fennel

½ head cauliflower

¼ head cabbage, ideally Caraflex, otherwise white

1 tablespoon Celery Salt (recipe follows)

2 tablespoons white wine vinegar

1 tablespoon lemon juice

4 tablespoons extra-virgin olive oil

1 small salami, fennel or piccante, thinly sliced

12 or more (depending on how many you like) Castelvetrano olives, pitted and pulled apart into halves

Very thinly slice the fennel, cauliflower, and cabbage either on a mandolin or with a knife to yield 4 cups. If your yield is higher, make sure to adjust the seasoning as needed.

In a large bowl, toss the vegetables with celery salt, white wine vinegar, lemon juice, and olive oil to evenly coat the vegetables. Let sit for a bit to allow the vegetables to soften up. Add the salami and olives, mix everything again, and serve.

CELERY SALT

¼ cup celery leaves

2 tablespoons kosher salt

In the bowl of a food processor, process the celery leaves until fairly well broken down, add the salt, and process further, until all the celery is pureed into the salt.

PUMPKIN, Castelfranco radicchio, and turmeric oil

SERVES 4

½ cup extra-virgin olive oil, plus more for roasting

1 tablespoon ground turmeric

1 chile de arbol

10 whole black peppercorns

1 bay leaf

1 small to medium red kuri squash

Kosher salt

¼ cup pumpkin seeds

1 bunch Castelfranco radicchio

Lemon

Sea salt

2 ounces Pecorino Toscano, for serving

Combine the olive oil, turmeric, chile de arbol, peppercorns, and bay leaf in a small saucepan. Stir to combine then place over low heat, stirring occasionally until fragrant and warm, about half an hour. Strain.

Preheat the oven to 400°F. Cut the squash in half, trim the ends, and scoop out the seeds. Cut the squash into ½-inch wedges. Toss the wedges in the turmeric oil (using only as much of the oil as you need to coat the squash), season with kosher salt, and roast on a sheet tray until the squash is caramelized and soft.

On a separate baking sheet, toss the pumpkin seeds with olive oil and salt and toast in the oven until they just start to turn golden, about 5 minutes.

In a large bowl, gently toss the radicchio and roasted squash with more of the turmeric oil, a squeeze of lemon, and a pinch of sea salt. Arrange on a platter, shave Pecorino Toscano generously all over the salad and sprinkle with the toasted pumpkin seeds.

TURNIPS AND RADISHES, butter and bottarga

SERVES 2 AS THE MAIN PART OF A MEAL, 4 AS A SIDE DISH

3 tablespoons extra-virgin olive oil

3 scarlet turnips, cut into halves or wedges

3 gold ball turnips, cut into halves or wedges

3 watermelon radishes, cut into halves or wedges

Sea salt

Black pepper

8 tablespoons unsalted butter

1 lemon

1 lump bottarga (cured mullet roe)

Warm the olive oil in a large pan over medium-high heat. Carefully add both the turnips and radishes to the oil. Allow the turnips to sit, undisturbed, in the pan to brown. Resist the temptation to move the turnips, but you can lift them up to check to see how they're doing. Once browned, shake the pan, move the turnips and radishes around, and add salt and pepper to taste.

Add the butter and lower the heat, allowing the vegetables to cook in the butter until tender, approximately 5 minutes. If the butter reduces too much or the pan becomes dry, add a little water to the pan.

Once the turnips and radishes are cooked, squeeze the lemon over them and toss to combine. Taste and season as needed. Transfer the turnips to a serving platter and generously shave the bottarga over the top.

"MINESTRONE," end-of-summer tomatoes and shell beans

SERVES 4

1 cup fresh cranberry beans (ideally) or other fresh shell bean

Extra-virgin olive oil

12 sage leaves

8 large garlic cloves, cut in half lengthwise

Kosher salt

4 cups cherry tomatoes

1 bunch spigarello or other seasonal green, such as spinach, Swiss chard, or kale, roughly chopped

Sea salt

Place the cranberry beans in a pot and add enough water to barely cover. Pour 2 tablespoons of olive oil over the beans and lay the sage leaves and garlic on top. Cook the beans at a gentle simmer adding water, a little at a time as necessary, until tender. Season the beans well with kosher salt.

Place the tomatoes on a sheet tray and drizzle with olive oil and salt. Roll the tomatoes around the tray to evenly cover them with the oil and salt. Broil the tomatoes until they char and wilt.

Add the tomatoes to the pot of beans.

In a sauté pan over medium heat, warm 3 tablespoons of olive oil until shimmering, and quickly sauté the spigarello until just wilted. Add the spigarello to the pot with the tomatoes and beans. Add water as necessary to desired consistency. Cook on low until the spigarello and the tomatoes melt into the soup. Season with sea salt to taste and serve.

CHICKEN SCHNITZEL
with butcher's cabbage

SERVES 4

CABBAGE

4 tablespoons extra-virgin olive oil

1 teaspoon mustard seed

1½ teaspoons coriander seed

1 small green chile, such as jalapeño or serrano, thinly sliced

1½ teaspoons ginger, peeled and grated

1 shallot, thinly sliced

1 teaspoon turmeric

1 small head white cabbage, thinly sliced

2 teaspoons kosher salt, plus more as needed

Juice of 1 lemon

SCHNITZEL

1 cup all-purpose flour

2 eggs, whisked

1½ cups bread crumbs

1 teaspoon kosher salt, plus more for seasoning the chicken

1 teaspoon cayenne, paprika, or dry mustard powder (optional)

4 boneless chicken breasts, pounded to approximately ¼ inch thick

Extra-virgin olive oil

To make the cabbage, warm the olive oil in a large-lidded saucepan over medium heat. Add the mustard and coriander seeds until they begin to pop. Add the chile and stir until fragrant. Add the ginger and shallot and cook, stirring constantly, until soft. Add the turmeric, stirring to ensure the spices don't burn, until the oil turns yellow. Add the cabbage and salt. Turn the cabbage in the pan to wilt a little and mix well with the spices. Turn the heat to low, cover the pot, and cook until the cabbage is wilted but still has some texture. Remove the pan from the heat and add the lemon juice. Season with salt to taste.

Set up a dredging station. Fill three bowls, one with flour, one with the whisked eggs, and one with the bread crumbs. Mix the flour with 1 teaspoon of salt and any seasoning spice you may choose (cayenne, paprika, or mustard). Dredge the chicken in the flour, shaking off any excess, then in the egg, then in the bread crumbs.

In a skillet over high heat, pour 1 inch of oil into the pan. When the oil reaches 325°F, fry the chicken cutlets until brown on both sides, approximately 3 minutes per side.

Drain the fried cutlets onto a cooling rack or paper towels and sprinkle with salt. Serve with the cabbage.

POACHED CHICKEN,
leeks, bacon, and prunes

SERVES 4

1 whole chicken

Kosher salt

1 bunch leeks, white and tender green parts, thinly sliced

3 tablespoons unsalted butter

1 cup pitted prunes

1 cup bacon lardons

Black pepper

Place the chicken in a stock pot and cover it with cold water. Add 2 tablespoons of salt and turn the heat to medium. Bring the water up to a boil and then remove the pot from the heat. Allow the chicken to cool completely in the pot before taking it out and pulling the meat off of the bones in large pieces. Strain the stock and set aside.

Sauté the leeks in butter in a medium pot over medium heat. Season with salt, add the prunes, and stir everything together. Add the chicken stock to cover the leeks and prunes and simmer until the prunes soften but don't get totally mushy. Add the pulled chicken and any additional stock to have your desired ratio of solids to liquid. In a separate pan over medium heat, cook the bacon until the lardons are caramelized and chewy.

Serve the chicken in shallow bowls with a grind of black pepper. Sprinkle the lardons on top of the plated soup.

PARSLEYED MEATBALLS, fregola

SERVES 4

MEATBALLS

1 bunch parsley, picked

¼ baguette, diced

6 tablespoons extra-virgin olive oil, plus more for tossing the bread

1 tablespoon kosher salt, plus more for tossing the bread

3 large garlic cloves

½ pound ground beef

½ pound ground pork

¼ cup (2 ounces) grated Parmigiano-Reggiano

4 tablespoons unsalted butter

Juice of 1 lemon

FREGOLA

Kosher salt

½ pound fregola

1 tablespoon unsalted butter

2 cups chicken stock

Wash and dry the parsley in a salad spinner. Reserve half for the bread crumbs and hold the other half to finish the dish.

Preheat the oven to 350°F. On a baking sheet, toss the baguette pieces with 3 tablespoons of olive oil and salt. Toast in the oven until deeply golden. Let the bread cool and dry out, then place in the bowl of a food processor and pulse until you have coarse crumbs. Add half of the parsley leaves and process into as fine a crumb as you can.

Make a paste with the garlic and 1 tablespoon salt. You can do this in a mortar and pestle or on a cutting board, as follows: Finely mince the garlic on a cutting board, and add some of the salt to the minced garlic. Make a paste by alternating between chopping the garlic and mashing it on the cutting board with the flat blade of your knife.

In a large mixing bowl, combine the beef, pork, garlic paste, any leftover salt from the original tablespoon, the bread crumbs, and Parmigiano-Reggiano and mix very well, really working the meat into a sticky paste. Form into walnut-sized meatballs.

In a large pan over medium-high heat, warm the olive oil until it shimmers. When the pan is hot, add the meatballs being careful not to overcrowd the pan. Once the meatballs start to brown, shake the pan to roll them around and brown on all sides. When the meatballs are brown and firm to the touch, add the butter and lemon juice to the pan along with a good amount of the remaining parsley.

In a pot of salted boiling water, cook the fregola as you would pasta. Once cooked, drain the fregola. Add it to a pot with the butter and enough chicken stock to cover it halfway and heat everything through.

To serve, place the fregola on a plate with a little of the liquid and then put the meatballs on top adding some of the pan juices to the plate.

LAMB BELLY,
potatoes, and tomatoes

SERVES 4

1 lamb belly, approximately
3 pounds

Kosher salt

Black pepper

1 teaspoon paprika

4 garlic cloves, thinly sliced

1 tablespoon picked rosemary,
plus a few sprigs

1 tablespoon picked thyme,
plus a few sprigs

2 large yellow onions, quartered

1 (28-ounce) can plum tomatoes,
drained of liquid

Extra-virgin olive oil

4 bay leaves

1 bottle white wine

4 to 6 Yukon gold potatoes,
peeled and cut into wedges

Juice of 2 lemons

3 tablespoons extra-virgin
olive oil

Sea salt

Lay the lamb belly out and season it well with kosher salt and black pepper on both sides. Sprinkle the paprika, garlic, rosemary, and thyme over both sides of the belly. Roll and tie the lamb belly with butcher's twine. Set aside.

Place the onions and tomatoes in a roasting pan large enough to hold the lamb. Season with salt and a generous drizzle of olive oil. Add the bay leaves and the sprigs of rosemary and thyme.

Preheat the oven to 300°F.

Place a quarter cup of olive oil in a large pan over medium high heat, and brown the lamb belly on all sides. Lay the browned lamb on top of the tomato and onion mixture, pour a ½ cup of the white wine into the roasting pan. Roast the lamb uncovered for 3 hours, until the lamb is very soft, and the vegetables and lamb have browned. Every 30 minutes, pour a little more white wine over the lamb. Toward the end, if the lamb gets too dark, cover it with foil. Remove the lamb from the oven and turn the oven up to 375°F.

In a separate roasting pan, toss the potatoes with the lemon juice, olive oil, and a pinch of sea salt. Lay the potatoes out on a single layer and roast until browned. If they are browning faster than they are cooking, move them around or add some water to the pan.

In the bowl of a food processor, puree the roasted tomato and onion mixture into a loose jam.

Serve the lamb with the jam, lemon potatoes, and the natural juices from the braise.

PORK CHOP, rutabaga, and sweet pickles

SERVES 2 TO 4

1 large rutabaga, peeled, and cut into 1-inch pieces

Kosher salt

8 tablespoons unsalted butter

2 thick-cut, bone-in pork chops

Black pepper

4 tablespoons extra-virgin olive oil

½ tablespoon Dijon mustard

½ tablespoon whole-grain mustard

½ cup white wine

½ cup chicken stock

¼ cup Bread and Butter Pickles (recipe follows)

Place the rutabaga and a teaspoon of salt in a large pot of water over medium heat. Bring to a boil and cook the rutabaga until it is tender when pierced with a knife. Strain the rutabaga and mash it with the butter. Taste and add salt as necessary. Set aside.

Season the pork chops on all sides with salt and pepper. Heat the olive oil in a large pan over medium heat. Sear the pork chops on both sides until deeply golden brown and until the pork reaches an internal temperature of 145°F. Remove the pork from the pan and set aside. Discard the oil from the pan.

In the same pan, stir in the Dijon and whole-grain mustards. Add the wine and chicken stock to the mustard and mix well. Heat the sauce on high, reducing it to make a clingy pan sauce.

Serve the pork chop with the rutabaga. Pour the sauce over all of it and serve with the pickles.

BREAD AND BUTTER PICKLES

½ cup cider vinegar

½ cup water

¼ cup sugar

2 tablespoons salt

1 teaspoon whole mustard seed

1 pound pickling cucumbers, sliced

Place the vinegar, water, sugar, salt, and mustard seed in a pot over high heat. Bring the mixture to a boil and add the sliced cucumbers to the liquid. Return the liquid to a boil before removing it from the heat. Let the cucumbers cool in the pickling juices before transferring it and its juices to an airtight jar. Refrigerate overnight.

GINGER CAKE, brown butter pears, and whipped cream

SERVES 12

1 cup unsalted butter, softened, plus more for the pan

3½ cups all-purpose flour, plus more for the pan

1 cup dark brown sugar

2 eggs

2 cups molasses

2 tablespoons ground ginger

2 teaspoons baking soda

2 teaspoons ground cloves

½ teaspoon salt

¼ cup minced candied ginger

1 cup boiling water

BROWN BUTTER PEARS

2 tablespoons unsalted butter

2 pears, cored, seeded, and cut into quarters or sixths

2 tablespoons sugar

Whipped cream, for serving

Preheat the oven to 350°F. Butter and flour a Bundt or loaf pan.

In the bowl of a stand mixer set with the paddle attachment or in a large bowl, cream the butter and the sugar on medium speed until well combined. Add the eggs one at a time, mixing well after each addition. Add the molasses in a steady stream, mixing to combine.

In a separate large bowl, sift the flour, ground ginger, baking soda, ground cloves, and salt. Stir in the candied ginger. Add the dry ingredients to the wet ingredients until just mixed. Add the boiling water a little at a time and mix well.

Pour the batter into the prepared pan and bake for 50 to 60 minutes, until a toothpick inserted in the center comes out clean.

To prepare the pears, melt the butter in a sauté pan over medium heat. Add the pears and sugar to the pan, tossing until the pears are soft and caramelized.

Serve the cake with the Brown Butter Pears and plenty of whipped cream.

PLUMS
with bread crumbs
and fresh cream

SERVES 4

8 plums, cut in half and
stones removed

8 tablespoons unsalted butter,
melted

2 tablespoons honey

1 loaf sourdough or other
hearty bread

1 tablespoon sugar

Cream

Preheat the oven to 350°F.

In a medium bowl, toss the plums with half of
the melted butter and all of the honey. Place
the dressed plums in either individual ovenproof
dessert bowls or into an ovenproof crock.

Cut the crust off the bread and either cut or tear
the bread into bite-sized pieces. In a medium bowl,
toss the bread with the remaining 4 tablespoons of
melted butter and the sugar. Place the large bread
crumbs on top of the plums in the roasting pan.
Bake for 10 to 15 minutes, until the plums bubble
and the large bread crumbs are toasty. Serve with
cold cream poured over the hot dish.

CITRUS SALAD
PORK RILLONS
GIZZARDS
POACHED FISH SALAD
STEAK TARTARE

STEAK + CAESAR
WHOLE FLUKE
BRAISED CHICKEN
SCALLOPS
SAUSAGES + POLENTA

VANILLA POT DE CRÈME
LEMON FOOL

CITRUS SALAD,
beets, and winter greens

SERVES 4

3 gold or Chioggia beets,
or a mix

Sea salt

2 blood oranges

1 oroblanco grapefruit

1 Cara Cara orange

1 tablespoon sherry vinegar

⅓ cup extra-virgin olive oil

4 cups bitter winter greens,
such as watercress, radicchio,
frisée, or escarole

¼ cup hazelnuts, toasted and
lightly crushed

Aleppo pepper or ground
chile de arbol

Place the beets in a medium pot, cover with water, and salt the water well. Cook the beets on high heat until tender when pierced with a knife. Cool the beets, peel them, and slice them into ¼-inch rounds.

Reserve one of the blood oranges for juicing. With the other blood orange, the grapefruit, and the Cara Cara orange, cut the top and bottom off of each fruit. Stand the citrus on your cutting board and then slice the peel away from the sides to remove all of the pith. Turn each citrus onto its side and cut into ¼-inch rounds to match the beets.

In a small bowl, juice the reserved blood orange and any collected juice from slicing the citrus. You should have about ¼ cup of juice. Add the sherry vinegar and olive oil and stir to combine.

Compose the salad on a platter by first laying down the greens and drizzling them with the dressing and a sprinkle of sea salt. Place down a layer of beets, then another drizzle of dressing, then the citrus, finally sprinkling the hazelnuts and chile on the top.

245

PORK RILLONS,
parsley salsa verde

SERVES 4

4 pounds skinned pork belly, cut into 2-inch cubes

2 tablespoons kosher salt

1 tablespoon black pepper

3 bay leaves

2 chiles de arbol, crushed

4 garlic cloves, cut in half

1 bottle red wine

Whole-grain mustard, for serving

Radishes, for serving

PARSLEY SALSA VERDE

1 cup picked parsley leaves

1 tablespoon capers

Juice from ½ lemon

1 tablespoon extra-virgin olive oil

If you have the time, toss the pork with the salt and pepper and let sit overnight in the refrigerator. If you don't have the time, don't be discouraged and make the rillons anyway.

Preheat the oven to 300°F. If the pork belly didn't sit overnight in the refrigerator, toss the pork belly cubes with salt and pepper. In a deep roasting pan, toss the seasoned pork with the bay leaves, chiles, and garlic. Add the wine to the pan and roast in the oven uncovered for 2 to 3 hours, stirring the pork periodically. The pork will cook slowly, releasing its fat. The wine will reduce, and eventually the pork will start to caramelize in its fat, becoming chewy and deeply browned.

To make the Parsley Salsa Verde, toss the parsley and capers with lemon juice and olive oil. Don't overdress or overwork the parsley; you want it to hold its shape.

Serve the pork belly with whole-grain mustard, radishes, and Parsley Salsa Verde.

GIZZARDS
à la frisée aux lardon

SERVES 4

GIZZARDS

1 pound duck gizzards

Kosher salt

Black pepper

¾ cup sherry vinegar

2 cups red wine

2 cups chicken stock

4 bay leaves

6 thyme sprigs

1 tablespoon whole black peppercorns

6 garlic cloves, cut in half

2 dried ancho or pasilla chiles, seeded and torn into pieces (optional)

SALAD

¼ cup extra-virgin olive oil, plus more for the pan

2 to 3 cups sourdough bread torn into large crouton-sized pieces

Sea salt

2 teaspoons Dijon mustard

2 tablespoons sherry vinegar

½ teaspoon grated garlic

White wine vinegar

4 eggs

1 large head frisée or chicory, washed and dried

Preheat the oven to 350°F. Season the gizzards with salt and pepper. Place them in a roasting pan with the vinegar, wine, stock, bay leaves, thyme, peppercorns, garlic, and chiles. Roast uncovered, stirring frequently, until tender, about 2 hours. The gizzards are done when they show no resistance when pierced with a knife. Set aside to cool in the braising liquid.

In a large sauté pan over medium high heat, add enough olive oil to just cover the bottom of the pan. Add the bread chunks and sprinkle with salt. Toss in the pan to cover the bread evenly and continue to stir the croutons until golden but still chewy.

Make a vinaigrette by mixing the mustard, vinegar, and garlic in a small bowl with a pinch of sea salt. Add the olive oil, stirring well to combine.

Bring a medium pot filled ⅓ of the way with water to a boil. Add a pinch of sea salt and a good splash of white wine vinegar to the water and lower the heat until the water is at a vigorous simmer. Crack 1 egg into a large spoon or small teacup. Stir the water in the pot into a whirlpool and slowly drop the egg into the simmering water. Repeat, adding all four eggs to the pot, one at a time. Cook the eggs until they float to the surface, making sure that they are not sticking to the bottom of the pan. Check the set of the yolk to determine when the eggs are done; they should start to firm up but not be too hard. Remove the eggs from the water and drain on a paper towel.

In a large pan on low heat, brown the gizzards in a pan until warmed through and a little caramelized.

To assemble, toss the frisée, gizzards, and croutons in a large bowl with the vinaigrette. Place the salad on individual plates and add a poached egg to the top of each salad.

POACHED FISH SALAD, pink celery

SERVES 4

1½ pounds fluke fillet or other flaky white fish

Kosher salt

¼ cup white wine

2 tablespoons extra-virgin olive oil, plus more as needed

2 bay leaves

4 thyme sprigs

1 lemon, juiced and 2 large strips of peel removed

6 whole black peppercorns

1 pink (or green if that's all there is) celery heart

Sea salt

1 garlic clove, thinly sliced

¼ cup parsley, sliced very thinly

Preheat the oven to 350°F.

Season the fluke lightly with kosher salt. Place the wine, olive oil, bay leaves, thyme, lemon peels, and peppercorns into a roasting pan. Place the seasoned fluke into the liquid and poach the fish in the oven, uncovered, for 15 to 20 minutes, until the whole fillet has evenly turned white and cooked through. Take the roasting pan out of the oven and leave the fish to cool in the liquid.

Slice the celery heart diagonally in ¼-inch slices. Make sure to include all the tender celery leaves. Dress the celery with a pinch of sea salt, some olive oil, and a squeeze of lemon.

Toss the fish very gently with 2 tablespoons of olive oil, 1 tablespoon of lemon juice, a pinch of sea salt, the sliced garlic, and the parsley. Place the fish on a platter and lay the dressed celery on top.

STEAK TARTARE,
parsley and capers

SERVES 4

1 tablespoon sherry vinegar

1 tablespoon minced shallot

Sea salt

2 tablespoons extra-virgin olive oil

1 pound top round steak, diced

1 to 2 teaspoons salt-packed capers, soaked and rinsed

1 tablespoon minced parsley

1 egg yolk

OPTIONAL GARNISHES

Cornichons

Dijon mustard

Toasted miche bread slices

Mix the vinegar, shallot, and a pinch of sea salt together in a small bowl. Let sit until the shallot softens and then add the olive oil.

In a large bowl, mix the diced top round with the vinaigrette and a sprinkling of sea salt. If you would like a more dressed tartare with a less strong taste of the beef, you can add more vinegar and olive oil. Mix in the capers and parsley and serve with an egg yolk and your desired garnishes on top.

STEAK AND CAESAR SALAD

SERVES 4

1½ to 2 pounds T-bone steak

½ teaspoon sea salt

Black pepper

Extra-virgin olive oil

¼ cup unsalted butter

CAESAR SALAD

3 tablespoons extra-virgin olive oil, plus more for the pan

2 to 3 cups sourdough bread torn into large croutons

Sea salt

2 garlic cloves

10 anchovy fillets

3 tablespoons Aioli (page 213)

Juice of 1 lemon

2 tablespoons white wine vinegar

4 ounces Parmigiano-Reggiano, shaved

2 heads mixed chicories

Preheat the oven to 400°F.

Season the steak well with salt and pepper. Heat a cast-iron skillet over high heat. Add the olive oil and sear the steak on both sides, about 5 minutes per side, until nicely browned. Transfer the pan to the oven until the steak reaches an internal temperature of 125°F. Remove the steak from the oven and transfer it to a plate to let it rest for 5 minutes. Pour the oil out of the pan. Once the steak is rested, add it back to the pan, and place it over medium heat. Add the butter to the pan and baste the steak with the browning butter until deeply browned. Slice and serve on a platter.

In a large sauté pan over medium heat, add enough olive oil to just cover the bottom of the pan. Add the bread chunks and sprinkle with salt. Toss the bread with the oil in the pan to cover it evenly and then stir the croutons until golden but still chewy.

Using a mortar and pestle, pound the garlic and salt as finely as you can. Add the anchovies and pound everything into a paste.

In a large bowl, combine the garlic paste, aioli, olive oil, lemon juice, white wine vinegar, and half of the shaved Parmigiano-Reggiano. Mix to incorporate. Toss in the chicories and coat well with the dressing. Add the croutons and continue tossing until everything is well dressed. Serve with additional shaved Parmigiano-Reggiano on top alongside the steak.

255

WHOLE FLUKE, brown butter, and capers

SERVES 2

1½ to 2 pounds whole fluke or flounder

Kosher salt

Extra-virgin olive oil

8 tablespoons unsalted butter

1 tablespoon salt-packed capers, soaked and rinsed

Juice of ½ lemon

Preheat the oven to 375°F.

Season the fish well on both sides with salt. Heat an oven-safe pan large enough to hold the whole fish over high heat. Add enough olive oil to just cover the bottom of the pan. When the oil is shimmering, lay the fish in the pan, skin side down. Cook the fish until golden brown and then, using a spatula, pull the fish away from the pan and flip it onto the other side. Transfer the fish into the oven for about 8 minutes to finish cooking.

Remove the fish from the pan and place it onto a serving plate. Discard the oil from the pan, add the butter, and place the pan back on the stove over medium heat, melting the butter until it sizzles and browns. Add the capers and lemon juice to the pan. Pour the butter over the fish and serve.

BRAISED CHICKEN, apricots, and tomatoes

SERVES 4

1 whole chicken

2 teaspoons ground cumin

2 teaspoons ground coriander

1 tablespoon sea salt

Extra-virgin olive oil

2 shallots, sliced

4 garlic cloves, smashed

1 cinnamon stick

8 dried apricots, sliced

6 whole peeled tomatoes (from a 14.5-ounce can)

Cut the chicken off the carcass and then into 8 pieces. Remove the wings. Place the chicken carcass and the wings in a pot and add just enough water to cover. Simmer for 1 hour.

Season the chicken pieces with the cumin, coriander, and salt. In another large pot over medium-high heat, add enough olive oil to cover the pan and brown the chicken pieces until the skin is crispy and golden. Remove the chicken pieces from the pot and set aside. Add the shallots, garlic, and cinnamon stick to the oil and sauté until soft and golden. Add the apricots and the tomatoes, breaking the tomatoes up with your hands.

Nestle the chicken pieces back into the pot and add enough of the chicken stock to come two-thirds of the way up the chicken. Simmer on low heat for 30 minutes. Serve immediately.

SCALLOPS, celery root purée, and Castelvetrano olives

SERVES 2

2 pieces celery root, peeled and cut into 1-inch pieces

¼ cup plus 3 tablespoons extra-virgin olive oil

Kosher salt

6 tablespoons unsalted butter, melted

8 dry diver scallops

Juice of 1 lemon

½ cup Castelvetrano olives, pitted

Smoked paprika

Preheat the oven to 350°F.

To make the celery root purée, toss the celery root with 3 tablespoons of the olive oil and a teaspoon of salt in a roasting pan. Cover the celery root with foil, and roast for about 40 minutes, until it becomes very soft. Remove the celery root from the oven and puree in a food processor. Add 4 tablespoons of the melted butter to the celery root as the machine is running, and season with salt as needed.

Season the scallops well with salt. Heat a pan large enough to hold all the scallops, add ¼ cup of the olive oil, and then sear the scallops over medium-high heat. Cook the scallops until they are nicely browned, 2 to 3 minutes, then flip the scallops and brown on the other side for another 2 to 3 minutes. Add 2 tablespoons of the butter and baste the scallops until they are deeply caramelized and the butter has browned. Pour the lemon juice over the scallops and into the brown butter.

Serve the scallops on top of the celery root purée, pouring the brown butter that remains in the pan over the purée. Sprinkle the olives around the plate and then lightly dust with smoked paprika.

SAUSAGES AND POLENTA, mushrooms

SERVES 4

4 salt-and-pepper or sweet Italian sausages

3 tablespoons extra-virgin olive oil, plus more for the pan

3 tablespoons unsalted butter, plus more as needed

2 large shallots, thinly sliced

4 garlic cloves, thinly sliced

Sea salt

8 thyme sprigs, picked

8 sage leaves, picked

4 cups mixed mushrooms, such as maitake, shiitake, and cremini, pulled apart or sliced into ½-inch slices

½ cup chicken stock

Black pepper

POLENTA

2 cups polenta

2 tablespoons kosher salt

8 tablespoons butter

Place the sausages in a large pan over medium heat and cover them halfway with water. Poach the sausages in the water for 10 minutes, making sure to flip the sausages over halfway. Once the water evaporates out of the pan, add a little olive oil, and cook the sausages until they are brown on all sides.

In a large sauté pan over medium-high heat, combine the olive oil and butter until the butter sizzles. Add the shallots and garlic with a seasoning of sea salt until they start to turn golden. Add the thyme, sage, mushrooms, and more salt, and cook on high heat until the mushrooms become brown and soft. Deglaze the pan with chicken stock and another spoon of butter and season with a few good turns of black pepper.

To make the polenta, bring a pot with 2 quarts of water to a boil. Whisk the polenta into the boiling water and add the kosher salt and butter. Cook the polenta, stirring often, for about 30 minutes.

Serve the mushrooms and sausages on top of the polenta.

VANILLA POTS DE CRÈME, preserved cherries

SERVES 4

1 cup milk

2 cups cream

6 egg yolks

¾ cup plus 2 tablespoons sugar

1 teaspoon vanilla extract

Amarena cherries or other preserved fruit of choice, for garnish

In a small pan over high heat, bring the milk and cream almost to a boil, and then remove it from the heat to cool to room temperature.

Preheat the oven to 350°F. Prepare four 6-ounce ramekins or teacups in a roasting pan.

In a large bowl, mix the yolks and sugar. Set aside.

Place the milk and cream in a small pan. Scald the milk and cream by bringing it almost to a boil over medium-high heat. Slowly whisk in the milk and cream mixture into the eggs, a little at a time, making sure not to scramble the eggs. Add the vanilla. Divide the mixture among the ramekins. Add hot water to the roasting pan until it comes two-thirds of the way up the sides of the ramekins. Cover the whole thing with foil and bake for about 30 minutes or until the pots de crème are just barely set all the way through to the center.

Remove the pots de crème from the oven, remove the foil, and let them cool in the water. Once fully cooled, refrigerate the pots de crème overnight, or at a minimum of 4 hours. Serve the pots de crème with the Amarena cherries.

LEMON FOOL

SERVES 4

6 eggs

1½ cups plus
1 tablespoon sugar

1 cup lemon juice

8 tablespoons cold
unsalted butter, diced

2 tablespoons
lemon zest

1 cup heavy cream

Whisk the eggs, 1½ cups sugar, and lemon juice in a double boiler over medium heat until well blended. Add the butter and lemon zest and cook for 20 minutes, whisking constantly, until the mixture is thickened. Transfer to a bowl to cool to room temperature. Cover with plastic wrap and refrigerate until cold, at least 2 hours.

In a small bowl, whip the cream with 1 tablespoon sugar and then fold the cream into the lemon curd. Don't completely mix in the cream; leave the mixture streaky. Serve immediately.

THE END
IS JUST THE
BEGINNING

KATE HULING

Having a restaurant, to me, feels the same as having a family: Once the initial fun spark is lit, the child or the restaurant embarks on its own journey of becoming, which has very little to do with the parents or the people who started it. The Diner has its own exquisite energy that is created and recreated every day. The bar, the stools, the tile, and booths are the same, but every day, it is its own collective energy, made up of cooks, porters, dishwashers, servers, bartenders, and managers, handypeople, office people, and customers. I look at the Diner with the same adoration and awe with which I look at my growing children—they are their own perfect vibrations, and I did not make them; they are not mine, they are their own. The Diner is its own.

We made this book because Julia Gillard's photos capture that phenomenal collective energy that is the Diner. It's a vibration that I never could express in words—you have to be there to know what I'm talking about—and Julia's photos are the next best thing.

Sitting down to write this conclusion for *Diner Day for Night,* I am naturally brought back to the moment when I was writing the introduction to *Dinner at the Long Table* in 2015. At that moment, Andrew and I were surrounded by a whole family of characters who had largely been with us for ten years or more, and there was this tremendous fullness to our lives. Our kids were four, seven, ten, and fifteen and a part of our everyday lives. The restaurants were filled with many of the same restaurant diners as the opening night of the Diner in '98.

Shortly after releasing the book, however, we experienced a massive and unprecedented exodus. Countless friends and restaurant regulars left Williamsburg, left NYC, left NY, and left the US. Most of the key players that I introduced in the *DATLT* introduction moved on from their posts at our restaurants: Dave to Japan, Jason to Upstate, Lee to California, Becky to Sweden, Sean to being a dad, Julia to full-time photography, Desi to study composting, Christina to Mexico City, Scarlet to Mexico City, and our beloved, South African Mark was diagnosed with a rare and deadly leukemia. Time passed, our older children started preferring their friends' company to our nightly family dinners, and I became overwhelmed with the sense of being left behind and falling apart. I think a lot of us experienced a deep sense of falling to pieces, and ultimately the need to find ourselves as individuals. Who were we apart from this all-consuming family of a community in Williamsburg?

Lee, Dave, and I—from California to Japan to Brooklyn—exchanged books that helped us through the process. Sean and I, who had always just shouted "hellos" to each other in passing, had the time to meet at the playground with our daughters and talk about social justice and the books we were reading. Caroline came back. While I was turning forty and going through my midlife crisis, she was turning fifty, and we shared how without foundation we both felt. Dave came back too and took a job working on a farm near us. He greeted us on Friday evenings with a warm fire and a pot of beans cooked with kombu. I started taking food to South African Mark while he was in treatment, and we would go on slow walks through Nolita.

All the while, Diner lived on, attracted new faces, new tastes in music, new jokes, new specials, and new farmers. Even though the people who I felt were so vital to the success of the restaurant were off having new adventures, the Diner didn't miss a beat. Liz, David, and Megan found us. Mason came back. Frank came back. People moved around and we made new relationships.

South African Mark passed on May 2, 2019, but he will never be gone from our lives. He visits us often in our dreams, and the way he shaped the spaces we occupy will always remain. Becky might live in Sweden, but she is teaching her son Arvid English so when he comes to NYC, he can tell us stories about his life in Sweden. AD will be a lawyer soon. They made us coffee, managed the Diner, and wrote *Diner Journals* and *DATLT*. They were an inextricable part of our every day, but in letting go of each other, they are finding the work that they were born to do. Tom B., to whom I will be forever grateful for not leaving at that time and for staying with us straight through the pandemic, has now started his new career. But his dance will go on forever. I will see his mambo and cha cha cha through the aisles of Roman's, Diner, and Marlow my whole life.

I used to not want to let go of anyone. I wanted everyone to stay forever, and even as I write this, my heart is burning, I have a lump in my throat, and my eyes are filled with tears, but now I understand that it is actually in people's leaving that we get to really love one another. The Diner is just the beginning for so many relationships, and Julia's photos and this book is a way for us to try to keep everyone together in one place. The burn of being splintered all over the globe is real, but seeing everyone's faces together in this book and chronicling the moments that we have shared together helps. Having these photos feels like putting all the pieces of us together again permanently, so there's a place for us all to live together yet again.

I have learned for myself, that no one ever really leaves, and nothing is ever lost. New faces and new characters come into our lives, new bonds are built, and even if we don't see the ones who have passed through these spaces every day, they are always with us. I want to say thank you to everyone who has come into our lives these past twenty-five years, to the ones who we still see every morning over coffee, or on the patio for a spritz (yes, you GT) and to the ones who always come to visit when they are passing through town. Our hearts are fuller than ever.

ABOUT THE CONTRIBUTORS

Caroline Fidanza is the culinary director of The Marlow Collective. She was the opening chef of Diner in 1999 and worked through the openings of Bonita, Marlow & Sons, Bonita 2, and Marlow & Daughters. She opened Saltie, a sandwich shop, in 2009, closed it, and rejoined the Collective in 2018. She is author of the *Saltie* cookbook and a regular contributor to *Diner Journal*.

Mark Firth, a laidback fifty-something with humor and drive, grew up in Zambia and traveled to Europe before moving to New York. There he worked for restaurateur Keith McNally and cofounded Brooklyn's preeminent Diner and Marlow & Sons. Mark now lives on an eighty-two-acre farm protected under agricultural conservancy and runs the Prairie Whale restaurant in Great Barrington.

Julia Gillard is a New York street photographer with a Midwesterner's eye for open spaces and the ways people bring life to the worlds they inhabit. Bartending weekends at Diner, she became inspired by and photographed the rhythms and rituals of daily life at the restaurant. During her tenure she served as photo editor for *Diner Journal*. Gillard's work has been exhibited at the New York Historical Society, the International Center of Photography, and the Brooklyn Museum. Her photographs have been published in *The New York Times, Mother Jones, The Wall Street Journal,* and *T* magazine and in the book, *Here Is New York*. Gillard is a visiting artist at Bard College and St. John's University.

Kate Huling is an entrepreneur and has been partner in crime to Andrew Tarlow since 1998. She still spends her time on Broadway at Shop Collective, which is the newest brick-and-mortar home for her leather goods and apparel brand: Marlow Goods. If you come to eat at Diner or Marlow & Sons, or to pick up groceries at Marlow & Daughters, make sure to stop in to say hi.

Becky Johnson is an art director and graphic artist who never tires of drawing letters and making dinner. In 2010, she moved to New York to pursue typeface design at Cooper Union for the inaugural year of Type@Cooper. She also hosted at Marlow & Sons and fell in love with the community on the corner. Before long, she became the art director for the *Diner Journal* and designed the group's first cookbook, *Dinner at the Long Table*. She now lives in Gothenburg, with her husband, Lars, a Swedish illustrator and their child, Arvid. Her work is based in New York with a focus on restaurants, food shops, and farm projects. beckprojekt.com.

Andrew Tarlow is widely recognized for pioneering the artisanal food movement in Brooklyn with his collection of acclaimed restaurants and businesses, including Diner, Marlow & Sons, Roman's, Achilles Heel, She Wolf Bakery, Marlow & Daughters, and Marlow Events. Tarlow is the author of *Dinner at the Long Table* and also the founder and publisher of *Diner Journal,* a quarterly magazine. Tarlow grew up in New York and began his career as a painter and bartender. He now lives in Fort Greene with his wife, designer Kate Huling, and their four children.

Published in the United States by Ten Speed Press, an imprint of Random House,
a division of Penguin Random House LLC, New York.
TenSpeed.com / RandomHouseBooks.com

Ten Speed Press and the Ten Speed Press colophon are registered trademarks of
Penguin Random House LLC.

Typefaces and lettering: Colophon Foundry's Aperçu; Milieu Grotesque's Maison Neue;
lettering on cover and menus by Becky Johnson; title in marker by Andrew Tarlow

Library of Congress Cataloging-in-Publication Data is on file with the publisher.

Hardcover ISBN: 978-1-60774-848-9
Ebook ISBN: 978-1-60774-849-6

Printed in China

Acquiring editor: Jenny Wapner | Project editor: Claire Yee
Editorial assistant: Gabby Urena | Production editor: Mark McCauslin
Designer: Becky Johnson | Design manager: Lizzie Allen
Food stylist & hand model: Ken Wiss
Production designers: Mari Gill and Faith Hague
Production manager: Serena Sigona
Copyeditor: Natalie Blachere | Proofreader: Lydia O'Brien
Publicist: Abdi Omer | Marketer: Chloe Aryeh

10 9 8 7 6 5 4 3 2 1

First Edition